MW00625809

ONE POT

WONDERFUL

The Perfect Pot

- is large enough to hold all ingredients with room to stir

- has oven-safe handles if it has to go from stovetop to oven or broiler

- can be used for both cooking and serving

ISBN-13: 978-1-56383-442-4
Item #7134

Printed in the USA by G&R Publishing Co.

Distributed By:

 Products

507 Industrial Street
Waverly, IA 50677

www.cqbookstore.com

gifts@cqbookstore.com

 CQ Products

 CQ Products

 @cqproducts

 @cqproducts

5 Reasons to Love
One-Dish Dinners

1 easy preps

2 fewer dishes to wash

3 layers of luscious flavor

4 unlimited variety

5 convenient cooking options

COOKING EVERYTHING in one pan suddenly makes mealtime simple! Whether you use the microwave, stovetop, oven, or slow cooker, these delicious dinners will fit any schedule or taste. Stuffed with veggies and other feel-good ingredients, it's comfort food's finest hour.

Convenient, versatile & scrumptious –
THIS IS ONE POT WONDERFUL!

4

Roasted Lemon Chicken & Veggies

Zest and juice of
  1 medium lemon

Olive oil

2 T. Dijon mustard

½ tsp. dried thyme

Salt and black pepper
  to taste

6 bone-in, skin-on
  chicken thighs

2 T. butter

1 to 1½ lbs. baby red
  potatoes, halved

1 lb. asparagus, green
  beans, or petite baby
  carrots

TO BEGIN, preheat the oven to 400°. Mix the lemon zest and juice, 2 tablespoons oil, mustard, thyme, salt, and pepper in a small bowl. Brush the mixture over both sides of chicken pieces.

Melt butter in a 12" oven-safe skillet over medium-high heat. Brown the chicken, about 3 minutes per side, until golden brown. Transfer to a plate.

Toss potatoes into the warm skillet with salt and pepper; roast uncovered in the oven for 20 minutes, until beginning to soften. Set chicken on top and roast uncovered 25 to 30 minutes more, until chicken is nearly done. Toss the asparagus with a little oil and tuck into skillet; roast uncovered 10 to 15 minutes longer, until everything is fully cooked and tender.

5

Saucy Pork Cutlets

Pound 4 (4 oz.) boneless pork chops to ¼" thickness. Cut 4 lemon slices in half and set aside. On a paper plate, mix 3 T. flour and ¼ tsp. each salt and black pepper; coat both sides of chops in the flour mixture. Heat 1 T. olive oil in a large nonstick skillet over medium-high heat and brown the chops 2 to 3 minutes on each side until golden brown. Move chops to the edge of the skillet and add set-aside lemon pieces; cook 1 minute on each side. Stir in 1½ C. chicken broth, ¼ C. rinsed capers, and 1 tsp. butter; simmer for 5 minutes. Add 2 C. fresh sugar snap peas and ¾ C. chopped fresh parsley. Simmer 3 to 4 minutes longer, stirring frequently, until peas are crisp-tender and chops test done with a meat thermometer *(145°)*.

Southwest Rice Skillet

Cook 1 lb. lean ground beef in a large skillet over medium-high heat until browned and crumbly; drain. Stir in 1 C. uncooked long-grain rice, 1 (10 oz.) can diced tomatoes with chiles, 1 (8 oz.) can tomato sauce, 1⅓ C. water, ½ C. diced bell pepper *(any color)*, 1 tsp. Southwestern chipotle seasoning, and ¼ tsp. red pepper flakes. Season with salt and black pepper to taste. Bring to a boil, then cover and reduce heat to low. Simmer for 25 to 30 minutes or until rice is tender and liquid is absorbed, stirring twice during cooking time.

Stir and sprinkle with 1 C. shredded Mexican or cheddar cheese. Remove from heat, cover, and let the cheese melt. Top with sour cream, diced tomatoes, cilantro, and sliced jalapeños before serving.

7

Short Rib Supper

2½ T. flour

2 tsp. each paprika and salt

¼ tsp. black pepper

2½ lbs. boneless beef short ribs *(about 5 pieces)*

1 to 2 T. olive oil

1 onion, chopped

3½ C. water

3 T. Worcestershire sauce

2 potatoes, peeled

2 or 3 carrots, peeled

3 small parsnips, peeled

2 celery ribs

½ C. uncooked quick barley

TO BEGIN, combine the flour, paprika, salt, and pepper on a paper plate and generously coat the ribs in the flour mixture. Heat the oil in a large pot over medium-high heat and brown the meat on all sides. Add the onion, water, and Worcestershire sauce. Bring to a boil, then reduce heat to low; cover and simmer slowly for 1½ hours, stirring occasionally.

Slice the potatoes, carrots, parsnips, and celery into ½" pieces. Add all the veggies to the pot, cover, and cook about 45 minutes, stirring occasionally. Stir in the barley and cook 15 to 20 minutes longer or until everything is tender.

SERVE WITH a loaf of hearty bread for a stick-to-the-ribs meal.

9

Tex-Mex Quinoa

1 T. olive oil

1 C. chopped onion

1 tsp. minced garlic

1 C. uncooked quinoa

2 (14.5 oz.) cans Mexican-style stewed or diced tomatoes

Water

1 T. ketchup or chili sauce

1 tsp. each ground cumin, ground oregano, and chili powder

Salt and black pepper to taste

1 (15 oz.) can black beans, drained & rinsed

1 (11 oz.) can whole kernel corn

3 C. fresh baby spinach

TO BEGIN, preheat the oven to 350°. In a large oven-safe skillet, heat the oil over medium heat. Add the onion and garlic; sauté about 8 minutes. Remove from heat and stir in the quinoa, tomatoes, ½ cup water, ketchup, cumin, oregano, chili powder, salt, and pepper until well combined. Cover tightly and bake about 30 minutes.

Remove from oven and stir in the beans and corn *(with liquid)*. Add ¼ to ½ cup more water as needed, then cover and bake 30 minutes longer. Before serving, stir in the spinach and let it wilt.

SERVE WITH sliced avocado, shredded Mexican cheese, or other favorite toppings.

The perfect accompaniment? A side of warm cornbread slathered with butter. Whether sweet or savory, it's a great addition to this meal.

11

Creamy Meatballs, Broccoli & Fries

In a 12" skillet, whisk together 1 (10.5 oz.) can cream of onion soup and ⅓ C. water. Add ½ (28 oz.) pkg. frozen steak fries *(partially thawed, about 3 C.)*; stir to coat. Bring to a boil over medium heat; reduce heat to low and simmer uncovered about 4 minutes, stirring occasionally. Stir in 3 C. frozen broccoli florets and about 26 fully cooked meatballs *(thawed, if frozen)*. Return to a simmer; cover the skillet and simmer gently for 10 to 15 minutes or until vegetables are tender. Stir in ¼ C. sour cream and cook just until heated through. Season with salt and black pepper. Dish up the goodness!

Glazed Salmon

Bring ½ C. chicken broth to a simmer in a large oven-safe skillet over medium heat. Arrange ½ lb. asparagus spears in skillet and set 2 (4 oz.) salmon fillets *(partially thawed, if frozen)* on top. Season with salt and black pepper. Cover and simmer 7 to 8 minutes, until fish is almost done and liquid has reduced by half. Meanwhile, preheat the broiler.

Mix ¼ C. seedless blackberry jam with 1 T. each olive oil and red wine vinegar, 1 tsp. each smoked paprika and ground cumin, and a dash of salt. Remove skillet from heat and spread a spoonful of jam mixture over each fillet; reserve remaining sauce. Broil the fish about 6" away from heat for 1 to 2 minutes or until glaze starts to bubble. Serve with the reserved sauce.

13

14

Sausage Ratatouille

1 medium eggplant

Salt

½ yellow onion

1 each red and green bell pepper, seeded

6 fingerling potatoes

1 jalapeño pepper, seeded

2 medium tomatoes

1 T. minced garlic

1 (19 oz.) pkg. Italian sausage links, sliced ½" thick *(remove skins as desired)*

½ C. chicken stock

1½ tsp. dried oregano

Red pepper flakes and black pepper to taste

TO BEGIN, cut the eggplant into 1" slices and sprinkle with 1½ teaspoons salt; let rest 15 to 30 minutes to "sweat." Blot the slices with paper towels, then cut into cubes and dump them into a greased 9 x 13" baking dish; set aside.

Meanwhile, preheat the oven to 400°. Thinly slice the onion, bell peppers, and potatoes; dice the jalapeño and tomatoes. Add these veggies to the baking dish, along with the garlic, sausage, stock, and oregano. Toss everything together and season with pepper flakes, salt, and pepper. Cover and bake about 45 minutes, until potatoes are tender and sausage is done.

15

SERVE WITH a fresh green salad and crusty bread.

Thai Chicken Soup

1 T. toasted sesame oil

2 tsp. each minced garlic and grated fresh gingerroot

1 lb. boneless, skinless chicken thighs, cut into 1" pieces

1 C. crushed tomatoes*

½ C. peanut butter

1 (49.5 oz.) can chicken broth (about 6 C.)

1 T. fish sauce

6 oz. uncooked rice noodles

2 C. shredded cabbage

1 C. canned bean sprouts, drained

¼ C. chopped green onion

TO BEGIN, heat the oil in a large pot over medium-high heat. Add the garlic, gingerroot, and chicken. Cook 3 to 5 minutes, stirring occasionally, until chicken is done.

Stir in the tomatoes, peanut butter, broth, and fish sauce and bring to a boil. Add the noodles and reduce heat; simmer for 5 minutes. Stir in the cabbage and cook 5 minutes more. Dump in the bean sprouts and green onion; stir and remove from heat. Let stand a few minutes before serving.

LADLE into bowls and dig in.

We pureed canned diced tomatoes in a blender.

Shrimp Scampi

1½ T. olive oil

2 T. minced garlic

¼ tsp. cayenne pepper

1 T. minced fresh oregano

3 T. minced fresh parsley

½ C. apple juice

½ tsp. sugar

1½ T. butter

2 C. chicken stock

¾ C. water

8 oz. uncooked linguini pasta

1½ lbs. large raw shrimp, peeled & deveined

1 tsp. lemon zest

2 to 3 T. lemon juice

8 cherry tomatoes, halved

¼ C. fresh basil leaves, chopped

Salt and black pepper to taste

18

TO BEGIN, heat the oil in a large deep skillet over medium-high heat. Add the garlic and sauté about 1 minute. Stir in the cayenne, oregano, parsley, apple juice, and sugar; cook for 1 minute. Stir in the butter until melted. Pour in the stock and water and bring everything to a boil.

Add the pasta and reduce heat to a simmer. Simmer uncovered for 8 to 10 minutes, stirring in the shrimp during the last 4 or 5 minutes, until pasta is al dente and shrimp turn pink. Stir in the lemon zest and juice, tomatoes, and basil. Season with salt and pepper, then let rest a few minutes to thicken sauce.

SPRINKLE WITH shredded Parmesan cheese and more fresh basil before serving.

You can't beat freshly grated Parmesan cheese to top off this scampi and lots of other main dishes - use generously!

19

Breakfast Skillet

In a 12" nonstick skillet, fry 6 bacon strips until crisp; drain and crumble the bacon, but reserve drippings in skillet. Sauté 1 C. chopped onion in drippings for 2 to 3 minutes. Stir in 6 C. shredded hash browns *(thawed)* and season with salt, black pepper, and garlic powder. Press potatoes into skillet to form a crust and cook on medium heat until golden brown and crisp on the bottom; flip crust onto a plate. Melt 1 T. butter in the skillet and cook other side of crust until lightly browned.

Make six wells in the crust and crack an egg into each one. Cover and cook on medium-low until eggs are set and cooked as you like. Sprinkle with shredded cheddar cheese, the crumbled bacon, and sliced green onion; cook until cheese melts.

Hearty Cabbage
& Kielbasa

Cut 1 (14 oz.) pkg. kielbasa sausage into ¼" slices.
Sauté in a 12" nonstick skillet until browned on both
sides; remove the meat and drain on paper towels.
Place 1 thinly sliced onion and 1 sliced green bell
pepper in the skillet and sauté 2 to 3 minutes. Add
6 C. chopped cabbage and cook about 8 minutes,
stirring often. Add the sausage, 1 C. chicken broth,
1 tsp. salt, and ½ tsp. each black pepper and caraway
seed. Reduce heat to medium-low and cook uncovered
for 10 minutes or until cabbage is tender. *(For a creamy
variation, stir in ¼ C. heavy cream before serving.)*

21

Scrape off gingerroot skin with the edge of a spoon.

Tangerine Beef

1 (1 lb.) beef flank steak

2 to 3 T. soy sauce

3 tangerines *(or 4 mandarin oranges)*

Vegetable oil

1 (12 oz.) bag fresh broccoli florets *(4 C.)*

1 red bell pepper, sliced

1 T. peeled & grated fresh gingerroot

¼ C. beef broth

2 T. cornstarch

2 T. hoisin sauce

TO BEGIN, slice steak across the grain into very thin strips; toss with the soy sauce and let rest. Meanwhile, peel off a thin layer of rind from one tangerine, removing any white pith. Slice the rind into narrow strips and set aside. Juice the two remaining tangerines and reserve ½ cup.

Heat 2 teaspoons oil in a large nonstick skillet over medium-high heat. Add the broccoli, bell pepper, gingerroot, and set-aside rind; cook and stir for 2 to 3 minutes. Push the food to one side of the skillet and add 1 tablespoon oil. When hot, add the beef; cook and stir until meat is lightly browned. Push the meat toward the other side of skillet and whisk in the broth, reserved juice, cornstarch, and hoisin sauce; bring to a boil while stirring. Reduce heat and stir everything together; simmer for a minute or two.

23

SERVE OVER rice or noodles if you wish.

24

Stovetop Greek Cod

4 (6 oz.) cod fillets
  (1" to 1½" thick)

Salt and black pepper
  to taste

2 T. olive oil, divided

½ C. sweet onion, sliced

2 C. sliced celery

½ tsp. anise seed

1 tsp. minced garlic

1 (14.5 oz.) can diced
  tomatoes

½ C. water

1 (14.5 oz.) can chickpeas,
  drained & rinsed

2 T. chopped fresh oregano

TO BEGIN, rub the fish fillets with salt and pepper. Heat 1 tablespoon oil in a 12" nonstick skillet over medium-high heat and brown the fish on one side only, 4 to 6 minutes; transfer to a plate.

Add the remaining 1 tablespoon oil to the skillet along with the onion, celery, and anise seed. Cook and stir over medium heat until crisp-tender, about 8 minutes. Add the garlic and cook 1 minute more. Stir in the tomatoes, water, chickpeas, and oregano; season with salt and pepper and bring to a boil. Reduce heat to maintain a simmer. Set the fillets into the sauce in the skillet, browned side up; cover and simmer 8 to 12 minutes or until fish tests done with a meat thermometer *(145°).*

GARNISH WITH lemon slices and fresh oregano.

Try this recipe with halibut or another white fish, too. Your exact cooking time will depend on the thickness of your fillets. Ours were 1" to 1½" thick.

25

Chinese Chicken Wraps

¼ C. toasted sesame oil, divided

1½ lbs. boneless, skinless chicken breasts, cut into 1" pieces

1½ tsp. minced garlic

2½ C. coleslaw mix or shredded cabbage, divided

1 (14 oz.) can bean sprouts, drained

1 (8 oz.) can sliced water chestnuts, drained

⅓ C. each hoisin sauce and soy sauce

¼ C. brown sugar

2 T. cornstarch

8 (8") flour tortillas, warmed

1 tomato, diced

Chow mein noodles

TO BEGIN, heat 2 tablespoons oil in a large skillet over medium-high heat. Add the chicken and garlic and cook for 8 to 10 minutes or until done, stirring frequently; pour off half the accumulated liquid in skillet. Stir in 2 cups coleslaw mix, bean sprouts, and water chestnuts. Cook about 4 minutes.

In a small bowl, whisk together the hoisin sauce, soy sauce, brown sugar, cornstarch, and remaining 2 tablespoons oil; pour into skillet and bring to a boil. Cook 1 minute to thicken.

Spoon some chicken mixture onto each tortilla and divide the remaining ½ cup coleslaw mix over the top. Sprinkle with diced tomato and some noodles. Roll up and enjoy!

28

Veggie Skillet Pizza

1 lb. loaf frozen whole wheat bread dough, thawed*

Olive oil

1 yellow bell pepper, diced

1 C. sliced fresh mushrooms

1 C. diced zucchini

2 green onions, sliced

¾ C. frozen chopped broccoli florets, thawed

Salt, black pepper, red pepper flakes, and Italian seasoning to taste

¾ C. pizza sauce

1½ C. shredded mozzarella cheese, divided

TO BEGIN, flatten dough into a 12" circle on a floured surface; set aside. Heat 1 tablespoon oil in a 12" oven-safe skillet over medium-high heat. Add all the vegetables and seasonings; cook until crisp-tender, stirring often. Transfer veggies to a bowl and preheat the broiler.

Reduce burner heat to medium-low and brush skillet with more oil. Press dough into skillet. Cook 12 to 15 minutes, until bottom is browned. Flip crust and spread with sauce. Sprinkle with 1 cup mozzarella, the cooked veggies, more Italian seasoning, and remaining ½ cup cheese. Cover and cook until cheese melts and crust is almost done, 10 to 15 minutes. Then broil pizza 7" away from heat for 3 to 5 minutes to brown the crust.

29

* Or, for a thin crust, use ½ loaf and shorten cooking time.

Slow 'n' Easy Meatball Stew

30

Thaw 1 (14 oz.) pkg. frozen fully cooked turkey meatballs *(about 26)* and dump them into a 3-quart slow cooker. Add 1½ C. frozen corn, 2 (14.5 oz.) cans Mexican-style stewed tomatoes, 1 (14 oz.) can chicken broth, 1 tsp. minced garlic, and 1 (15 oz.) can black-eyed peas or pinto beans *(drained & rinsed)*. Cover and cook on low 6 to 7 hours *(or on high for 3 to 3½ hours)*. Ladle into bowls and garnish with corn chips and fresh oregano. Mmm...

Skillet Mostaccioli

Preheat the oven to 475°. Combine 1 T. olive oil,
1 T. minced garlic, ½ tsp. red pepper flakes, and
½ tsp. salt in a large oven-safe nonstick skillet over
medium-high heat; cook about 1 minute. Stir in
1 (28 oz.) can crushed tomatoes, 3 C. water, and 12 oz.
uncooked mostaccioli or other tubular pasta *(about
3 ¾ C.)*. Cover and simmer 15 to 18 minutes, stirring
often, until pasta is almost tender. Stir in ½ C. heavy
cream, ½ C. grated Parmesan cheese, and 3 T. chopped
fresh basil; season with salt and black pepper. By small
spoonfuls, drop ½ C. ricotta cheese over the pasta
mixture and sprinkle with 1 C. shredded mozzarella.
Transfer skillet to the oven and bake 10 minutes or
until cheese is lightly browned. Cool slightly and top
with more basil.

31

32

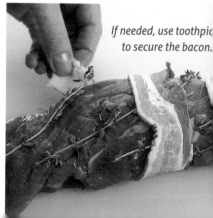

If needed, use toothpic
to secure the bacon.

Bacon-Wrapped Pork

1 (1 lb.) pork tenderloin

Salt and black pepper

4 sprigs fresh thyme

4 bacon strips

2 T. olive oil, divided

1 lb. new red potatoes,
   cut into wedges

½ onion, thinly sliced

¼ C. apricot jam

12 dried apricots, halved

½ C. apple juice

TO BEGIN, preheat the oven to 400°. Pat the tenderloin dry with paper towels and sprinkle with ½ teaspoon each salt and pepper. Top the pork with thyme and wrap with bacon strips; set aside.

Heat 1 tablespoon oil in a large oven-safe skillet over medium-high heat. Add the potatoes, season with salt and pepper, and cook about 5 minutes, stirring often, until beginning to brown and soften. Push potatoes to one side of skillet. Heat the remaining 1 tablespoon oil and add the onion and set-aside pork. Brown the meat about 2 minutes on all sides and stir potatoes and onions often.

Brush meat with jam, then add apricots and juice to the skillet. Transfer skillet to the oven and roast uncovered for 20 to 25 minutes or until pork tests done with a meat thermometer (145°). Let rest at least 5 minutes before slicing.

33

Sheet Pan Chicken Dinner

1 large sweet potato, peeled
    & cut into 1" chunks

¾ lb. red potatoes,
    cut into 1" chunks

¾ lb. Brussels sprouts,
    trimmed *(halved, if large)*

6 oz. shallots, peeled
    & halved

6 garlic cloves, peeled
    & halved

1 T. olive oil

2 T. minced fresh thyme

1 tsp. sugar

Salt and black pepper

1 (3½ to 4 lb.) chicken,
    cut into pieces

2 T. butter, melted

2 tsp. minced fresh rosemary

*Peel off and discard the
sprouts' outer leaves.*

34

TO BEGIN, preheat the oven to 475° and line a large sheet pan with foil. Combine the sweet and red potatoes, Brussels sprouts, shallots, and garlic on the prepared pan and drizzle with oil; toss to coat. Sprinkle with thyme, sugar, ¾ teaspoon salt and ¼ teaspoon pepper and toss again. Spread the veggies in a single layer.

Season chicken with salt and pepper and arrange over the vegetables. Brush the chicken with butter and sprinkle with rosemary. Roast uncovered for 35 to 40 minutes or until chicken tests done with a meat thermometer *(165°)*. Rotate the pan once during cooking time. Remove from oven, tent food loosely with foil, and let rest 5 to 10 minutes before serving.

GARNISH WITH more fresh rosemary if you'd like.

Strip the leaves off rosemary or thyme stems by pinching the top of the stem with one hand and sliding the fingers of your other hand down the stem from top to bottom. Easy!

35

Lemon Shrimp Risotto

1 T. butter

2 tsp. olive oil

⅓ C. chopped red onion

1 (12 oz.) pkg. uncooked Arborio rice *(scant 2 C.)*

Zest and juice of 2 large lemons

2 (14 oz.) cans chicken broth

½ C. apple juice

12 to 16 oz. raw shrimp, peeled & deveined

1 C. frozen peas

¾ tsp. salt

¼ tsp. black pepper

TO BEGIN, combine the butter, oil, and onion in a 3- to 3½-quart microwaveable bowl. Microwave uncovered on full power for 2 minutes or until onion softens. Stir in the rice and microwave on full power 1 minute more.

Add 1 tablespoon lemon zest, ¼ cup lemon juice, broth, and apple juice; stir well and cover the dish. Cook on 50% power for 18 to 20 minutes, stirring twice, until most of the liquid is absorbed. Stir in the shrimp, peas, salt, and pepper. Cover and cook on 50% power for 3 to 4 minutes longer, stirring once, until shrimp turn pink and rice is tender.

GARNISH WITH any remaining lemon zest and some fresh parsley.

37

Remove the entire shrimp
shell, including tail.

Cheesy Skillet Ravioli

1 T. olive oil

1 lb. ground Italian sausage

1 (14.5 oz.) can diced tomatoes with garlic & olive oil

1 (8 oz.) can tomato sauce

1 T. tomato paste

1½ tsp. Italian seasoning

1 tsp. each garlic powder and onion powder

Salt and black pepper to taste

16 oz. frozen cheese ravioli

1 C. water

1 C. shredded mozzarella cheese

⅓ C. grated Parmesan cheese

TO BEGIN, heat the oil in a large oven-safe skillet over medium-high heat. Add the sausage and cook until browned and crumbly; drain. Stir in the tomatoes, tomato sauce, tomato paste, and all seasonings. Stir in the ravioli and water and bring to a boil. Cover the skillet, reduce heat, and simmer until ravioli is tender, 10 to 12 minutes. Meanwhile, preheat the broiler.

Remove skillet from heat and stir; sprinkle with both cheeses. Transfer skillet to broiler and broil ravioli about 6" away from heat until just golden brown, 2 to 4 minutes.

SPRINKLE WITH fresh basil before serving.

Grand Gumbo

6 to 9 oz. fully cooked
   Andouille sausage, sliced

1 C. chopped celery

1 green bell pepper,
   chopped

½ C. chopped onion

2 tsp. minced garlic

½ C. canola oil

½ C. flour

4 C. chicken stock

2 (14.5 oz.) cans stewed
   tomatoes, coarsely
   chopped

2 C. frozen cut okra, thawed

1 lb. boneless, skinless
   chicken thighs

1 T. smoked paprika

4 to 6 oz. fully cooked
   peeled shrimp (thawed,
   if frozen)

Salt and black pepper
   to taste

1½ to 2 C. cooked rice,
   optional

*Use two forks to shred the
cooked chicken easily.*

TO BEGIN, brown the sausage in a large pot over medium heat about 4 minutes. Remove to a bowl, reserving drippings in the pot. Add the celery, bell pepper, onion, and garlic to pot and cook for 8 minutes, stirring occasionally, until veggies are crisp-tender. Dump them in with the sausage and reserve for later use.

Heat the oil in the same pot over medium heat and gradually whisk in the flour. Cook and stir for 6 to 8 minutes or until mixture turns medium brown. Gradually whisk in the stock. Stir in the tomatoes, okra, chicken, paprika, and reserved sausage mixture. Bring to a boil, then reduce heat, cover, and simmer for 40 minutes, stirring occasionally.

Remove chicken and shred; return the shredded meat to the pot along with the shrimp. Season with salt and pepper and heat through. Ladle into a bowl and add a scoop of rice if you'd like.

SERVE WITH French bread. Isn't that grand?

41

For a surprising citrus kick, stir 1 teaspoon orange zest into the rice before adding it to the soup. Gumbo yumbo!

Smothered Chicken

Preheat the oven to 350°. Dump 1 (10 oz.) pkg. plain couscous into a greased 9 x 13" baking dish. Stir in 2 C. water and 1 T. olive oil; spread evenly and let stand 5 minutes.

Rinse and coarsely chop 1 (2.25 oz.) jar sliced dried beef and scatter over couscous. Top with 6 boneless, skinless chicken breast halves and season with black pepper. Mix 1 (10.75 oz.) can cream of chicken soup and 1 C. sour cream; spread evenly over ingredients in dish. Sprinkle with ¼ C. cooked crumbled bacon. Cover and bake 40 minutes; uncover and bake 10 minutes longer or until chicken is fully cooked. Lightly stir the couscous and serve with the chicken.

Slow Cooker Chinese Beef

In a 3-quart slow cooker, mix 1 C. beef broth, ½ C. soy sauce, ⅓ C. brown sugar, 1 T. toasted sesame oil, and 2 tsp. minced garlic. Add 1 lb. very thinly sliced boneless beef chuck roast *(or flank steak)* and toss until coated. Cover and cook on low for 5 to 6 hours.

Mix 2 T. cornstarch with 2 T. cold water; slowly stir into slow cooker. Add ½ C. sliced green onion, 1 C. sliced fresh mushrooms, and 1½ C. each petite baby carrots and fresh green beans *(choose thin ones or parcook them first)*. Stir, cover, and cook on high about 1½ hours more, until sauce is thickened and vegetables are crisp-tender. Can be served over noodles.

43

Turkey & the Works

- 2 lemons
- 1 C. chicken broth
- 1 (8 lb.) bone-in turkey breast
- 1 T. butter, melted
- 1 C. water
- 2 lbs. small Yukon gold potatoes, halved
- 1 lb. butternut squash, peeled & cut into 1" chunks
- 8 small to medium beets, peeled & quartered
- 1½ to 2 (8 oz.) pkgs. small white boiling onions, peeled
- 1 T. dried basil

TO BEGIN, preheat the oven to 350°. Coat a 10 x 15" roasting pan and rack with cooking spray and set rack inside. Thinly slice one lemon and juice the remaining one. Mix 2 tablespoons juice with broth and set aside.

Loosen the turkey skin and slide lemon slices underneath. Set turkey on the rack and brush with butter. Add water to pan and roast the turkey uncovered for 1¼ hours.

Remove from oven and increase oven temperature to 375°. Arrange all vegetables around the turkey. Pour set-aside broth mixture over everything, then sprinkle with basil. Roast uncovered for 1 to 1½ hours longer or until turkey tests done with a meat thermometer (165°) and vegetables are tender. Let stand 15 minutes before carving.

45

Don't be afraid to lift up that turkey skin!

46

Ham & Potato Pot Pie

2 T. butter

1 C. chopped onion

3 leeks, sliced & rinsed

4 medium Yukon gold potatoes, cubed

2 C. frozen peas and carrots

2 T. flour

1¼ C. chicken stock

1½ C. cubed ham

⅓ C. sour cream

2 tsp. whole grain mustard

Salt and black pepper to taste

2 bay leaves, optional

4 Grands Flaky Layers refrigerated biscuits *(from a 16.3 oz. tube)*

1 egg, beaten

TO BEGIN, preheat the oven to 400°. In a large oven-safe skillet over medium heat, melt the butter. Add the onion and leeks, cover, and cook for 5 minutes. Stir in the potatoes; cover and cook 10 minutes more, until veggies are fork-tender and browned. Stir in the peas and carrots and cook just until warmed.

Sprinkle flour over the vegetables and stir in the stock until combined. Bring to a boil and cook about 2 minutes to thicken. Remove from heat and stir in the ham, sour cream, and mustard. Season with salt and pepper and add the bay leaves, if using. Split biscuits in half and arrange over the filling; brush tops with egg. Bake 14 to 18 minutes or until biscuits are deep golden brown and filling is bubbly. Discard the bay leaves before enjoying.

Spicy Orange Chicken

½ C. flour

4 tsp. cornstarch

¾ tsp. garlic powder

1½ tsp. onion powder

1 lb. boneless, skinless chicken breasts, diced

Olive oil

¾ C. tomato sauce

1½ tsp. orange zest

3 T. orange juice

⅓ C. chicken broth

3 T. brown sugar

2 T. minced garlic

1 T. each Sriracha sauce and soy sauce

¼ tsp. each red pepper flakes and black pepper

1 C. frozen shelled edamame

1 (8 oz.) can sliced water chestnuts, drained

¼ C. sliced green onion

48

TO BEGIN, combine the flour, cornstarch, garlic powder, and onion powder in a large zippered plastic bag and shake to mix. Add the chicken and shake until well coated. Heat about 2 tablespoons oil in a large skillet over medium heat, and working in batches, shake excess flour off chicken and sauté until browned and cooked through, adding more oil as needed. Remove chicken to a plate as it is done.

Wipe out the skillet and add the tomato sauce, orange zest and juice, broth, brown sugar, garlic, Sriracha, soy sauce, pepper flakes, and pepper. Stir well and simmer over medium-low heat for 5 minutes. Add the edamame, water chestnuts, and onion; cook about 2 minutes more. Stir in the chicken and cook until sauce thickens and everything is hot, 2 or 3 minutes longer.

SERVE OVER rice, noodles, or couscous if you'd like.

Garnish any main dish with angled slices of green onion. Use the darkest parts for the biggest impact.

Deli Stovetop Pizza

Olive oil

1 small yellow onion, thinly sliced

Salt and red pepper flakes

1 to 2 tsp. minced garlic

1 (11 to 13.8 oz.) tube refrigerated pizza crust

8 oz. fresh mozzarella cheese, thinly sliced

4 oz. thinly sliced deli meats, chopped (we used salami, ham & pastrami)

⅓ C. grated Parmesan cheese

Chopped fresh parsley

TO BEGIN, heat 1 tablespoon oil in a 12" oven-safe skillet over medium-high heat. Add the onion and sprinkle with ½ teaspoon each salt and pepper flakes. Sauté until onions soften and begin to brown; transfer to a plate. Preheat the broiler.

Brush the warm skillet with 1 tablespoon oil, then unroll dough and press it over the bottom of pan. Reduce burner heat to medium and cook 2 to 3 minutes, until the bottom of crust is golden brown; flip the crust. Reduce heat to medium-low and brush browned side of crust with more oil and garlic; sprinkle with salt. Arrange mozzarella slices on crust and scatter prepped onions all over. Top with meats, Parmesan cheese, and pepper flakes. When bottom of crust is golden brown, broil pizza 7" away from heat until cheese is bubbly and crust is brown, about 3 minutes.

Quick Hamburger Stew

Thaw ½ C. frozen green beans, ¾ C. frozen corn, and 2 C. frozen stew vegetables *(our blend contained potatoes, carrots, celery, & onion)*; set aside. Crumble 1 lb. lean ground beef into a microwaveable colander set over a 2-quart microwaveable dish. Microwave on high about 5 minutes, stirring once, until meat is crumbly and no longer pink. Discard fat and wipe out dish; let meat cool.

In the same dish, mix 1 (1.5 oz.) pkg. beef stew seasoning and 2 T. flour. Whisk in 2 C. warm water and 2 tsp. instant beef bouillon. Stir in beef and vegetables. Cover and microwave on high about 9 minutes, stirring every 3 minutes, until vegetables are done to your liking. Let stand a few minutes to thicken.

Easy Enchilada Bake

Preheat the oven to 350°. In a big oven-safe skillet over medium-high heat, cook 1 lb. lean ground beef until browned and crumbly; drain. Stir in 2 to 3 tsp. taco seasoning, 1 C. black beans *(drained & rinsed)*, 1 C. frozen corn, 1 C. mild enchilada sauce, and ½ C. tomato sauce. Separate the biscuits from a 7.5 oz. refrigerated tube and cut each into four equal pieces. Stir the biscuit pieces into the beef mixture and spread evenly in skillet. Sprinkle with 1 C. shredded Mexican cheese and bake for 25 to 30 minutes or until golden brown and bubbly. Garnish with fresh cilantro before serving.

53

54

Creamy Corn & Chicken Skillet

1½ lbs. chicken tenders
  (*unbreaded*)

Salt and black pepper
  to taste

¼ C. butter, divided

⅓ C. white wine vinegar

6 green onions, sliced
  (*reserve dark slices*)

⅓ C. chicken broth

1 (16 oz.) pkg. frozen corn,
  thawed & drained

4 oz. cream cheese, cut
  into pieces

½ C. milk

TO BEGIN, season the chicken with salt and pepper. Melt 2 tablespoons butter in a 12" skillet over medium-high heat. Add the chicken and brown both sides, 5 to 7 minutes, pouring off excess liquid as needed.

Stir in the vinegar, scraping up any browned bits; simmer about 1 minute. Push chicken to one side of skillet and melt the remaining 2 tablespoons butter. Add the white and pale green onion slices and sauté 1 minute. Stir in the broth and simmer 3 or 4 minutes or until chicken is cooked through, turning often to coat in sauce. Add the corn and cook several minutes, until heated through. Add cream cheese and milk; cook and stir until cheese melts and everything is hot and creamy. Sprinkle with salt, pepper, and reserved onion slices.

Skillet Chops & Apples

4 boneless pork chops
(¾" to 1" thick)

Salt, black pepper, and
garlic powder to taste

1 T. coconut oil

4 Braeburn apples,
peeled, cored & sliced

1 small fennel bulb, cored
& coarsely chopped

½ yellow onion, thinly
sliced

1¼ C. chicken broth

1 tsp. ground cinnamon

1 bunch fresh kale, stems
removed & leaves
chopped

¼ C. raisins

TO BEGIN, preheat the oven to 400°. Pat chops
dry with paper towels and season both sides with
salt, pepper, and garlic powder. Heat the oil in a large
oven-safe skillet over medium heat and add the chops;
brown 2 to 3 minutes on each side. Add the apples,
fennel, and onion. Cook until apples begin to soften,
stirring frequently. Stir in the broth and cinnamon;
simmer 2 to 3 minutes.

Transfer skillet to the oven and cook uncovered for
7 to 10 minutes, until chops test done with a meat
thermometer (145°). Remove chops to a plate to keep
warm. Add kale and raisins to the skillet; stir and
cook until kale is slightly wilted and raisins are warm.
Return chops to the skillet, heat through, and serve.

57

Use a nice sharp knife to cut the fennel.

One-Pot Turkey Dinner

8 oz. herb-seasoned stuffing cubes

½ C. hot water

2 T. butter, sliced

¾ C. chopped onion

1 (4 oz.) can sliced mushrooms, drained

¼ C. dried sweetened cranberries

3 boneless, skinless turkey breast fillets *(about ¾ lb. each)*

½ tsp. each salt and black pepper

¾ tsp. dried basil

¼ tsp. poultry seasoning

6 carrots, peeled & cut into 1" chunks

2 T. butter, softened

TO BEGIN, coat a large slow cooker with cooking spray *(we used a 5-quart oval cooker)*.

Dump the stuffing into the cooker and add the water, sliced butter, onion, mushrooms, and cranberries; stir well.

Cut each turkey fillet in half and sprinkle with salt, pepper, basil, and poultry seasoning. Arrange the fillets in a single layer on top of the stuffing mixture in cooker and place carrots around the edge. Cover and cook on high 3¼ to 4 hours *(or on low for 7 to 8 hours)*, until carrots are crisp-tender and turkey tests done with a meat thermometer *(165°)*. Remove turkey and carrots, and toss the carrots with softened butter. Fluff up the stuffing mixture and let everything rest a few minutes before serving.

SERVE WITH sliced oranges or cranberry sauce and a side of pumpkin bread – your delicious Thanksgiving dinner is ready!

60

Sweet Potato Corn Chowder

- 1 (12 oz.) pkg. fully cooked Andouille chicken sausage, diced
- 1 C. each chopped onion and chopped celery
- 1 T. minced garlic
- 3 T. flour
- 1½ tsp. each ground cumin and chili powder
- 1 tsp. Cajun seasoning
- 6 C. chicken broth
- 1 (16 oz.) pkg. frozen corn
- 2 C. peeled & diced sweet potatoes
- ¾ lb. boneless, skinless chicken breasts, cut into ¾" pieces
- 1 C. heavy cream
- 1 tsp. black pepper
- Tortilla strips, optional

TO BEGIN, brown the sausage in a large Dutch oven over medium heat, stirring occasionally. Add the onion, celery, and garlic; cook and stir for 5 minutes. Stir in flour, cumin, chili powder, and Cajun seasoning and cook 2 minutes more, tossing frequently. Stir in the broth and bring the mixture to a boil.

Add the corn, sweet potatoes, and chicken. Return to a boil and then reduce heat. Cover and simmer about 20 minutes or until potatoes are tender and chicken is done. Stir in cream and pepper, then cook until hot. Sprinkle tortilla strips on top to add crunch.

61

Spinach-Artichoke Pasta

Thaw and drain 1 (10 oz.) pkg. frozen chopped spinach; press well to remove excess liquid and set aside.

Cook 14 oz. rigatoni pasta in boiling water as directed on package, 13 to 15 minutes. Drain and return pasta to the pot. Over low heat, stir in ¼ C. milk, 2 C. shredded Monterey Jack cheese, ½ C. shredded Parmesan cheese, and 3 T. butter until everything is melted. Add the set-aside spinach and 1 (14 oz.) can artichoke hearts *(drained & chopped)*; stir to combine. Season with salt and black pepper and heat through. Sprinkle with more Parmesan or French fried onions if you'd like.

Easy Beef Stir-Fry

In a Dutch oven or large skillet, cook 1½ lbs. ground beef with 1 tsp. minced garlic over medium heat until browned and crumbly; drain and transfer to a bowl.

In the same pan, heat 1 T. vegetable oil over medium-high heat. Add 1 sliced red bell pepper, 2 C. sliced fresh mushrooms, and 4 oz. trimmed fresh pea pods; stir-fry for 3 to 4 minutes, until crisp-tender. Return beef to the pan along with 3 C. cooked rice *(use leftovers or packaged ready-rice)*, ½ C. soy sauce, and ¼ tsp. ground ginger. Cook 4 to 5 minutes or until heated through, stirring often. Reduce heat to medium and add 2 beaten eggs; cook and stir until eggs are done. Sprinkle with sliced green onion before serving.

63

Index